THE
HEALTHY
HEART
COOKBOOK

Jill Bradley

Sweetwater Press
Florence, Alabama

Published by Sweetwater Press
P.O. Box 1855
Florence, Alabama 35631

Produced by The Triangle Group, Ltd.
227 Park Avenue
Hoboken, NJ 07030

Design: Tony Meisel
Special thanks to Risa Gary of Mikasa, New York
Origination and printing: Cronion S.A., Barcelona

Printed in Spain

ISBN 1-884822-00-2

Contents

Introduction

A healthy heart is one of the most important goals in any diet. After all, you only have one and, though replacements are available, they are not something you can rely on.

Fat, salt, fried foods and sugar are not good for your heart (or for much else, either). By inference, very little fast food is good for you, since most of it is fried and loaded with fats and sodium.

The American Heart Association has published dietary guidelines for maintaining your heart in peak condition:

1. The amount of fat you eat should be less than 30% of your total calories.
2. Saturated fats should be less than 10% of your daily calories.
3. Polyunsaturated fat should be less than 10% of your daily calories.
4. Cholesterol should be less than 300 milligrams a day.
5. Complex carbohydrates should make up 50% of the daily intake.
6. Proteins should make up the remainder of the daily intake.
7. Sodium should be less than 3000 milligrams per day.
8. Alcohol should be limited to no more than 2 ounces of 100 proof whiskey, 8 ounces of wine or 24 ounces of beer.
9. Your total caloric intake should be sufficient to maintain your recommended body weight.
10. Your diet should be balanced, with many different nutrients.

Of course, none of this should be undertaken lightly. You need sound nutritional and medical advice at all times. You also need to exercise.

The recipes herein are designed to maintain a low cholesterol level. They are also as devoid of fats, sodium and sugars as possible consistent with good taste and the chemistry of cooking. Small amounts of fats and other so-called bad foods cannot harm you, so long as you don't go overboard. Binging of any kind puts an enormous strain on the heart. Moderation is the key to a healthy heart.

Small Red Potatoes with Chives

24 very small new potatoes, unpeeled
boiling water
1 cup plain non-fat yogurt
3/4 cups chopped chives and/or imitation bacon bits

Wash and dry the potatoes. Place the potatoes into a large saucepan with enough boiling water to cover them. Quickly bring the water back to boil, then reduce the heat and cook until the potatoes are tender but still firm, about 10 minutes.

Drain the potatoes and immediately drop them into a bowl of cold water. When the potatoes are cool, drain again and pat dry. Cut a thin slice from the bottom of each potato so that they will stand upright in a dish.

Using a spoon or melon baller, scoop out a small cavity in each potato. Fill the cavities with the plain yogurt and top with chopped chives, imitation bacon bits or both. Serves 6 to 8.

Fresh Salmon Paté

1 pound fresh, boned salmon fillet
1 teaspoon salt substitute
1/2 teaspoon fresh peppercorns
2 tablespoons fresh lemon juice
1 tablespoon chopped fresh tarragon
1 small white onion
1 medium boiled potato, peeled and quartered
1 teaspoon fresh peppercorns
1/2 cup plain non-fat yogurt
non-fat crackers and toast points

Place the salmon fillet in a saucepan with water to cover,
salt substitute and 1/2 teaspoon fresh peppercorns. Bring
the mixture to a boil, lower the heat and cover and simmer for 15 to 20 minutes or until the salmon flakes easily.
Let the salmon come to room temperature in the water.
Drain, skin and flake.

In a food processor or blender combine the salmon,
lemon juice, tarragon, onion, potato, fresh peppercorns
and non-fat yogurt. Process until smooth. Transfer the
mixture into a mold that has been sprayed with non-fat
cooking spray or into ramekins. Cover and chill over-
night. Serve surrounded with crackers and toast points.
Serves 6 to 8.

Chicken Soup with Greens & Mushrooms

2 tablespoons low fat or non-fat margarine
1/2 cup finely chopped chives
2 cups fresh spinach, washed and torn into pieces
1/2 cup fresh mushrooms, sliced
1/4 cup dried mushrooms, chopped
4 cups non-fat chicken broth
freshly ground black pepper
salt substitute

In a medium size saucepan melt the margarine over a high heat. Add the chives, spinach and fresh mushrooms. Sauté until vegetables are wilted, approximately 4 minutes.

Transfer mixture with a slotted spoon to a saucepan. Add the dried mushrooms and the chicken broth. Heat thoroughly to combine flavors and season according to taste. Serves 4.

Squash Soup

4 cups peeled and cubed butternut or acorn squash
1/4 teaspoon cinnamon
4 cups non-fat chicken broth
1 cup non-fat yogurt
1 tablespoon freshly grated nutmeg
freshly ground black pepper

In a large saucepan combine the squash, cinnamon and chicken broth, bring to a boil. Lower the heat and cover, cook gently for 25 to 35 minutes or until the squash is done.

Transfer the mixture to a food processor or blender, purée until smooth. Return the purée to the saucepan, if it is too thick add water and cook until heated through. Ladle into soup bowl and top with yogurt, nutmeg and black pepper.

Fennel, Arugula & Orange Salad

1 medium-size fennel bulb with stalk,
    trimmed and washed
1 fresh lemon
2 bunches fresh arugula, trimmed and washed
2 seedless oranges, peeled, sliced and cut into pieces

Dressing
6 tablespoons vegetable or olive oil
3 tablespoons orange juice
1/4 teaspoon mustard
freshly ground black pepper to taste

Slice the bulb and stalk of the fennel into rings and place in a large bowl. Sprinkle with the juice of 1 fresh lemon, toss and allow to stand for 15 minutes.

Add arugula to the fennel, and if the leaves are too large, tear them in half. Add the orange slices. Season with freshly ground pepper.

In a small bowl combine the oil, orange juice, mustard and pepper. Whisk until well blended. Pour over the salad mixture, toss and serve. Serves 4.

String Bean & Tomato Salad

2 pounds string beans, ended and washed
4 ripe fresh tomatoes
2 cloves garlic, crushed
coarsely ground black pepper
Vinaigrette:
4 tablespoon olive oil or vegetable oil
2 tablespoons white wine vinegar or lemon juice
1/2 teaspoon Dijon mustard

In a large pot of boiling water blanch the string beans until just tender, approximately 5 to 8 minutes. Remove from the heat, drain and rinse with cold water.

Coarsely chop the tomatoes and transfer them to a large mixing bowl. Add the string beans and the garlic to the tomatoes, season with pepper.

In a small jar combine the oil, vinegar or lemon juice and mustard, shake well. Pour over the beans and toss well; adjust seasonings. Allow to marinate for 2 hours. If you refrigerate this, return it to room temperature before serving. Serves 6-8.

Tangy Mixed Vegetables

1 pound new potatoes
1 cup broccoli flowers
3 bell peppers (1 each red, orange and yellow)
1 medium zucchini
1 large red onion, sliced very thin and broken into rings
Dressing:
4 tablespoons olive oil or vegetable oil
2 tablespoons red wine vinegar
1 tablespoon non-fat plain yogurt
2 teaspoons Dijon mustard
1 clove garlic
2 tablespoons fresh thyme leaves or chopped tarragon
freshly ground black pepper

Scrub the potatoes and cut into bite-size pieces, steam in a pot of boiling water until just tender, about 5-8 minutes. Remove from the heat and transfer to a large bowl.

Steam the broccoli flowers until just tender, about 5-7 minutes. Remove from the heat and cool briefly. Transfer to the bowl with the potatoes.

Halve, core and wash the peppers. Cut them into bite-size chunks and add to the bowl with the potatoes and broccoli.

Wash the zucchini and slice very thin; add to the bowl. Add the red onion.

In a food processor, blender or jar combine the ingredients for the dressing. Process or shake well. Pour over the vegetables and season with pepper. Toss well. Cover and allow to marinate for 2 hours. If you refrigerate this, return it to room temperature before serving. Serves 10.

Steamed Root Vegetables

1 package fresh baby carrots or 3 thin carrots
4 small turnips
1 medium rutabaga
2 tablespoons vegetable oil
2 cloves fresh garlic, crushed
coarsely ground black pepper
2 tablespoons fresh Italian parsley, chopped

Wash the carrots and slice into thin strips. If using regular carrots cut each carrot into quarters and then slice.

Peel the turnips and the rutabaga and cut into thin slices, cut each slice into thin strips.

In a pot of boiling water cook the vegetables all together until crisp-tender; this should not take more than 3 minutes. If some are done before others, transfer them with a slotted spoon to a bowl. When all the vegetables are done, transfer to strainer, drain and place in the bowl.

In a medium skillet heat the oil, add the garlic and cook briefly. Add the drained vegetables and toss until coated and hot. Add the pepper and parsley, toss again. Remove from the heat and serve. Serves 4-6.

Steamed Cauliflower
with Pepper Purée

2 red bell peppers
1 head of cauliflower, washed and separated
    into bite-size pieces
2 teaspoons olive or vegetable oil
freshly ground black pepper
1 tablespoon fresh thyme

Preheat oven to broil. Place peppers in oven and roast for 8-10 minutes, turning twice, until charred. Carefully remove from oven and transfer to a brown paper bag, close and let peppers rest for 5 minutes. Remove the peppers and carefully peel the skin off. Cut the tops off and core. Transfer to a food processor or a blender. Add the oil and process to a thick purée.

    In a large pot of boiling water cook the cauliflower until tender, approximately 5-8 minutes.

    While the cauliflower is cooking transfer the purée to a saucepan. Add the black pepper and thyme and cook until heated.

    When the cauliflower is done, drain and transfer to a bowl. Drizzle the pepper purée on top and toss or serve on the side as a dip. Serves 4-6.

Stuffed Sweet Peppers

4 large bell peppers (red, yellow or orange)
3 tablespoons olive or vegetable oil
1 large onion, sliced
1 cup dried currants
1/2 cup pine nuts
2 cups brown rice, cooked according
    to package instructions
1 cup no-salt chicken broth, flavored with black pepper
    and chopped garlic

Preheat the oven to 375 degrees F.
    Cut the tops off the peppers and set aside. Hollow out
the peppers and rinse well.
    In a large skillet heat the oil, add the onion and sauté
until translucent. Add the currants and pine nuts. Cook
for an additional minute.
    Add the cooked rice to the skillet and gently mix until
coated.
    Place the chicken broth, pepper and garlic in the
bottom of a casserole large enough to hold the four
peppers.
    Stuff the peppers with the rice mixture and transfer to
the casserole, gently place the tops back on the peppers.
Place in the oven and bake for 30 to 45 minutes, or until
peppers are tender.
    When ready to serve, transfer to a platter, remove the
tops from the peppers and spoon the broth-garlic mixture
over each pepper. Serves 4.

Steamed New Potatoes with Mint

1 pound small new or red potatoes
2 teaspoons non-fat margarine
3 tablespoons freshly chopped mint
freshly ground black pepper

Wash the potatoes, do not peel.

In a pot of boiling water cook the potatoes until just tender, approximately 8 minutes.

While the potatoes are cooking, slowly melt the margarine in a small saucepan.

When the potatoes are done, drain and return to the pot. Pour the melted margarine over them, then the mint and black pepper. Toss gently and transfer to a bowl. Serves 4-6.

Sautéed Sweet Potatoes with Shallots

2 pounds sweet potatoes
6 tablespoons non-fat margarine
8 shallots, quartered
3/4 cup non-fat chicken broth
salt substitute, to taste
freshly ground black pepper to taste

Peel the potatoes and cut them into 1/4 inch slices. Cut each slice into quarters.

Melt 3 tablespoons of the margarine in a large skillet over a moderately high heat. Add half the sweet potatoes and sauté until they are light brown, about 8 to 10 minutes. Remove the sweet potatoes from the skillet and put them in a bowl. Add 2 more tablespoons of the margarine to the skillet and cook the remaining potatoes as above. Add them to the potatoes already in the bowl.

Melt the remaining tablespoon of margarine in the skillet over moderate heat. Add the shallots and sauté until light brown, about 6 to 8 minutes. Stir in the chicken broth and simmer the mixture, stirring often, until the shallots are cooked and glazed, about 5 minutes.

Raise the heat to moderately high and return the sweet potatoes to the skillet. Cook until they are golden brown and heated through, about 5 minutes. Use a spatula to turn the potatoes. Be sure they heat and brown evenly.

Remove the sweet potato mixture from the skillet and transfer to a serving dish. Serves 4 to 6.

Lemon Rice

1 cup long-grain white rice
3 tablespoons non-fat margarine
salt substitute, to taste
freshly ground black pepper to taste
2 tablespoons fresh lemon juice
1/4 cup black olives, pitted and chopped
1 teaspoon finely grated lemon rind

Bring 4 cups of water to a boil in a large saucepan. Add the rice, and cook over a high heat, stirring often until the rice is just tender, about 15 minutes. Remove the rice from the heat and drain in a colander. Rinse with cold water and drain again.

Melt 1 tablespoon of the margarine in a large skillet over a low heat. Add the rice, salt substitute and black pepper. Heat the rice, fluffing it with a fork. When the rice is hot, add the lemon juice, olives, and lemon rind. Stir gently for 5 seconds, then remove from the heat. Add the remaining margarine (if needed) and stir gently. Serves 6.

Spicy Brown Rice

1 tablespoon non-fat margarine
1 large white onion
2 cups uncooked brown rice
3 cups water
2 cups non-fat chicken broth
2 cloves garlic, crushed
2 teaspoons chili powder

In a large skillet melt the margarine over a moderately high heat. Add the onion and sauté for 2 minutes. Add the garlic and sauté 1 minute longer. Add the rice and chili powder and cook 2 minutes longer.

Add the water and chicken broth. Bring the mixture to a boil, reduce the heat to a simmer and cook covered for 35 to 40 minutes or until the rice is tender. Just as the rice has absorbed all of the liquid you may wish to turn it off and place a piece of paper towel over the top and then cover again. This will help absorb extra moisture. Serves 6 to 8.

Linguine with Tuna Sauce

1 tablespoon olive or vegetable oil
1 large white onion, chopped
2 cloves garlic, chopped
1/4 cup chopped fresh basil
1 large can Italian tuna in olive oil, drained
1 large can imported Italian plum tomatoes, drained
2-4 drops of Tabasco sauce
freshly ground pepper to taste
1 pound linguine

In a medium-size saucepan heat the oil, add the onion and garlic and cook only until wilted and translucent.

Add the basil, tuna and tomatoes to the saucepan, stir to combine. Season with Tabasco, pepper and cook over a low heat until sauce is hot and flavors are combined, approximately 15 minutes.

While the sauce is simmering, cook the pasta in a large pot of boiling water until it is *al dente*. Drain well.

Transfer the pasta to a large serving dish and spoon the sauce over the pasta. Toss gently but well. Serves 4.

Pasta with
Raw Tomato Sauce

4 ripe tomatoes at room temperature
1/2 cup chopped fresh basil
4 cloves fresh garlic, finely chopped
1/2 teaspoon hot red pepper flakes
freshly ground pepper to taste
1/2 cup olive or vegetable oil
1 pound vermicelli or thin spaghetti

Coarsely chop the tomatoes and put them into a large nonmetal bowl. Add the basil, garlic, red pepper flakes and black pepper. Stir until well mixed. Add the olive oil and toss gently. Let the mixture stand at room temperature for 2 hours to blend flavors. Toss occasionally.

Cook the pasta in a large pot of boiling water until it is *al dente*. Drain well.

Put the pasta in a serving bowl. Pour the tomato mixture over the pasta and toss gently but well. Serves 4.

Lime-Ginger Grilled Tuna

1/2 cup fresh lime juice
2 cloves fresh garlic, finely chopped
2 tablespoons olive oil
2 tablespoons vegetable oil
salt substitute, to taste, if desired
freshly ground black pepper to taste
1 1/2 teaspoons finely chopped fresh ginger
1 teaspoon slivered lime rind
6 fresh tuna steaks, about 1-inch thick

Combine the lime juice, garlic, olive oil, vegetable oil, salt substitute, pepper, ginger and lime rind in a mixing bowl. Whisk until well blended.

Put the tuna steaks in a shallow dish large enough to hold them in one layer. Pour the marinade over the fish. Turn the steaks to coat well. Cover the dish and marinate in the refrigerator for 4 hours, turn occasionally.

Preheat the broiler or gas grill or prepare a charcoal grill.

Remove the tuna steaks from the marinade, reserve the marinade. Grill the steaks 3 inches from the heat until lightly browned, 3 to 5 minutes per side.

Put the reserved marinade into a saucepan and gently heat until hot.

Arrange steaks on a serving platter and pour hot marinade over each. Serves 6.

Grilled Swordfish

1/4 cup fresh lime juice
1/4 cup fresh lemon juice
1 teaspoon grainy mustard
1 clove of garlic, crushed
1/4 cup fresh tarragon, chopped
1/2 cup olive or vegetable oil
4 swordfish steaks, about 1 inch thick
coarsely ground black pepper

In a blender or in a jar combine the lime juice, lemon
juice, mustard, garlic, tarragon and oil, process or shake
until well mixed.

Place the swordfish steaks in a large shallow plate,
pour the marinade over the steaks, turn to coat and
season with black pepper. Cover and marinate for at least
2 hours, turning occasionally.

Preheat the broiler or gas grill, or prepare a charcoal
grill. Remove the steaks from the marinade. Grill the
steaks 3 inches from the heat source for approximately
3 to 5 minutes per side or until done. Serves 4.

Spiced Broiled Salmon

1 tablespoon olive or vegetable oil
1 tablespoon Mongolian Fire oil or sesame oil
1 tablespoon dried orange peel
1/2 teaspoon coarsely ground black pepper
1 teaspoon chopped garlic in oil
2 pounds salmon fillet

In a shallow dish combine the olive oil, Mongolian Fire oil or sesame oil, dried orange peel, black pepper and garlic; stir to mix.

Cut the salmon fillet into 4 equal pieces. Place the fish skin side up into the marinade, turn to coat and then let marinate with the skin side up for at least 2 hours at room temperature.

Preheat the oven to broil. Lightly spray a broiling pan with low-calorie cooking spray.

Place the fish, flesh side up, on the broiling pan. Broil gently for 10 to 15 minutes depending on the thickness of the fish. Do not turn. Fish will be charred and crispy outside, moist inside. Serves 4.

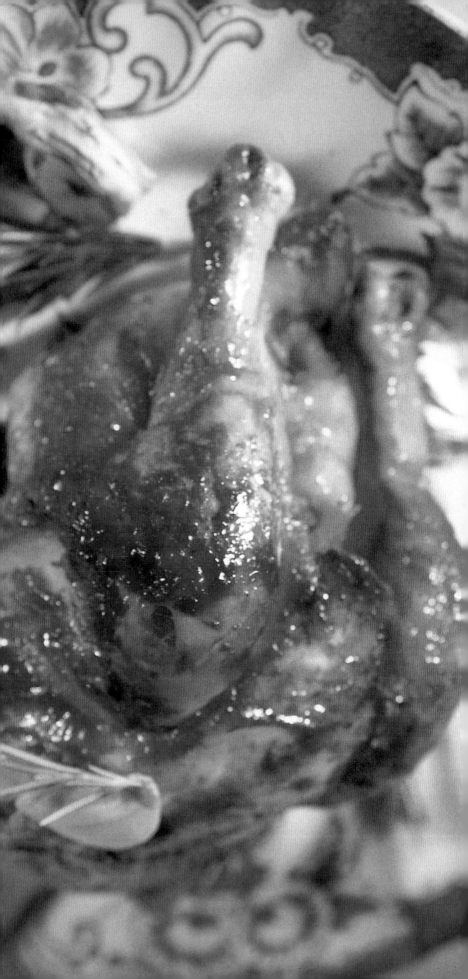

Roast Chicken

1 roasting chicken, 3 to 4 pounds
2 tablespoons fresh rosemary
2 teaspoons chopped garlic in oil
1 heaping teaspoon Dijon style mustard
1 tablespoon olive or vegetable oil
coarsely ground black pepper
1 tablespoon non-fat margarine
1 large white onion.

Preheat the oven to 425 degrees F. Have a roasting pan and non-stick roasting rack ready.

Wash the chicken inside and out, pat dry.

In a small bowl combine the rosemary, chopped garlic, mustard, olive oil and pepper, mix to form a paste. Set aside.

Cut the onion into chunks small enough to fit inside the chicken, any leftover can be placed around the chicken as it roasts. Place the onion chunks in the chicken along with the margarine. Truss or skewer the chicken closed.

Carefully place the chicken on a cutting board coated with waxed paper. Cover the entire chicken with the herb mustard paste. Sprinkle with additional black pepper. Transfer to the roasting rack.

Place in the oven and roast for 20 minutes at 425 degrees F. Turn the oven down to 375 degrees F. and continue roasting until done, approximately 1 to 1 1/4 hours, depending upon your oven. If you wish, you may baste the chicken with additional margarine that has been melted while it is roasting, but this may not be necessary.

Remove from the oven and let rest for 15 minutes before slicing. Remove the skewers or cord and spoon out the onions. Serves 4.

Chicken Fricassee

1 3-pound chicken
2 medium onions, cut into large chunks
2 cloves garlic, minced
1 tablespoon chopped fresh basil
1 can imported Italian plum tomatoes
4 small new potatoes, washed and diced
1/2 cup water
1/2 cup white wine
1/2 cup coarsely chopped mushrooms
freshly ground black pepper
salt substitute to taste

Cut the chicken into serving pieces and remove the skin and all visible fat.

Into a large pot place the chicken, onions, garlic, basil, tomatoes with the liquid, from tomatoes, potatoes and water. Allow the mixture to come to a boil, cover and reduce heat. Cook gently for 40 to 45 minutes. Add the mushrooms and wine and cook for an additional 5 minutes. Serves 4.

Grilled Marinated Chicken

1 3-pound chicken
2 tablespoons olive or vegetable oil
1 heaping teaspoon chopped garlic in oil
1 tablespoon fresh rosemary
1/4 cup fresh lime juice
2 tablespoons Dijon-style mustard
freshly ground pepper to taste

Cut the chicken into serving pieces, remove the skin.

In a large bowl combine the olive oil, garlic, rosemary, lime juice, mustard and pepper, whisk to blend. Add the chicken pieces to the bowl and turn them 3 or 4 times until well coated, season with additional pepper. Cover and allow the mixture to marinate at room temperature for 3 to 4 hours.

Preheat the oven to broil or a gas grill or ready a charcoal grill. Spray the boiler pan or the grill with low-calorie olive oil cooking spray.

Place the chicken in the broiler or on the grill and cook, turning often for approximately 35 to 45 minutes or until tender. Serves 4.

Chicken-Vegetable Kabobs

2-3 pounds boneless, skinless chicken breast
1/4 cup light soy sauce
2 tablespoons Mongolian Fire oil or sesame oil
2 cloves garlic, chopped
1 large white onion, cut into chunks
3 bell peppers; red, orange and yellow, cut into chunks
1 box button mushrooms, washed

Cut the chicken breast into large cubes.

In a large bowl combine the soy sauce, Mongolian Fire oil and garlic, blend with a spoon or fork. Add the chicken pieces and turn to coat. Cover and allow to marinate at room temperature for at least 2 hours.

Preheat the broiler or gas grill or prepare a charcoal grill.

Using 4 large metal skewers, alternately arrange the chicken, onion, peppers, and mushrooms on the skewers. Grill for 20 minutes, turning often, or until vegetables and chicken are tender. Serves 4.

Roast Cornish Hens

2 tablespoons olive or vegetable oil
1 large white onion, chopped
2 teaspoons chopped garlic in oil
1 pound button mushrooms, washed and sliced
2 cups cooked brown rice
1 teaspoon dried thyme
freshly ground black pepper
4 Cornish game hens
4 tablespoons non-fat margarine, at room temperature
black pepper
salt substitute

Preheat the oven to 400 degrees F. Have roasting pans and racks ready to hold 4 game hens.

In a large skillet heat the oil, add the onions and garlic and sauté until the onion becomes translucent. Add the mushrooms and cook until the mushrooms begin to soften, stir occasionally. Add the cooked rice and mix well. Cook until heated through, season with the thyme and black pepper.

Spoon the rice mixture into the hens and skewer closed. Any leftover rice can be served on the side with the meal. Spread 1 tablespoon of margarine on the out-side of each hen, season with black pepper and salt substitute.

Roast hens for approximately 40 to 45 minutes or until juices run clear. Remove skewers. Serves 4.

Turkey Scallops

2 pounds turkey cutlets
flour for dredging
2 tablespoon olive or vegetable oil
4-6 tablespoons non-fat margarine
salt substitute
freshly ground black pepper to taste
1/2 pound fresh mushrooms, thinly sliced
1/2 cup dry white wine
3/4 cup low-fat chicken broth
3 tablespoons fresh lemon juice
2 tablespoons chopped parsley
2 lemons, sliced paper-thin

Put the turkey cutlets between two sheets of waxed paper and lightly pound them with a meat mallet or the side of a heavy knife or cleaver. Dredge the slices in the flour, shaking off any excess.

Melt 2 tablespoons of the margarine with the oil together in a large skillet over moderately high heat. When very hot, add as many turkey cutlets as will fit comfortably. Sauté the slices until browned, about 1 to 2 minutes per side. Remove the slices from the skillet and keep warm on a plate. Season with black pepper and salt substitute if desired. Cook the remaining turkey as above.

Melt 2 more tablespoons of the margarine in the skillet. Add the mushrooms and sauté stirring constantly for 3 to 4 minutes. Add the wine, chicken broth and lemon juice. Stir well and bring the mixture to a boil. Continue to boil until the sauce is slightly thick, about 3 minutes. Add the remaining margarine (if desired) and whisk to blend. Add the chopped parsley and additional salt substitute and pepper to taste. Stir well.

Return the turkey to the skillet and cook until heated through. Transfer the turkey to a serving platter and spoon sauce over the slices. Top with lemon slices.
Serves 6 to 8.

Turkey Curry

3 tablespoons non-fat margarine
2 cups cubed cooked turkey
1 large onion, chopped
1 teaspoon chopped garlic in oil
1 cup low-fat chicken broth
2 teaspoons curry powder
1 tart apple, chopped
1 cup raisins
1/2 cup water, if needed
non-fat plain yogurt

Melt the margarine in a large skillet, add the chicken, onion and garlic. Sauté until the chicken is evenly brown.

Add the chicken broth and curry powder, stir well. Add the apple and raisins. Cook gently, stirring occasionally for 10 minutes or until the flavors are mixed and the curry is a good consistency. Add the water only if it is too thick. Serve atop rice with plain yogurt. Serves 4.

Grilled Pork Chops

1 16-ounce container non-fat yogurt
2 tablespoons chopped garlic in oil
2 tablespoons fresh rosemary,
    plus 3 sprigs fresh rosemary
coarsely ground black pepper
4 thick center cut pork chops, all visible fat removed

In large bowl combine the yogurt, garlic, 2 tablespoons of rosemary and black pepper, mix well. Add the pork chops and turn several times until well-coated, place rosemary sprigs on top. Cover and let marinate at room temperature for 4 hours.

Preheat broiler or gas grill or ready a charcoal grill.

Remove the chops from the yogurt mixture, making sure they are still well-coated. Grill 3 inches from the heat source for 3-6 minutes a side or until golden and no longer pink inside. Serves 4.